Winter in Nunavut

WRITTEN BY
Maren Vsetula

2

Nunavut is an exciting place in the winter. Even though the days can be cold, there is still so much to see and do!

In the winter, people usually travel by snowmobile. Large parts of the Arctic Ocean freeze. It is even possible to drive on the ocean in the winter!

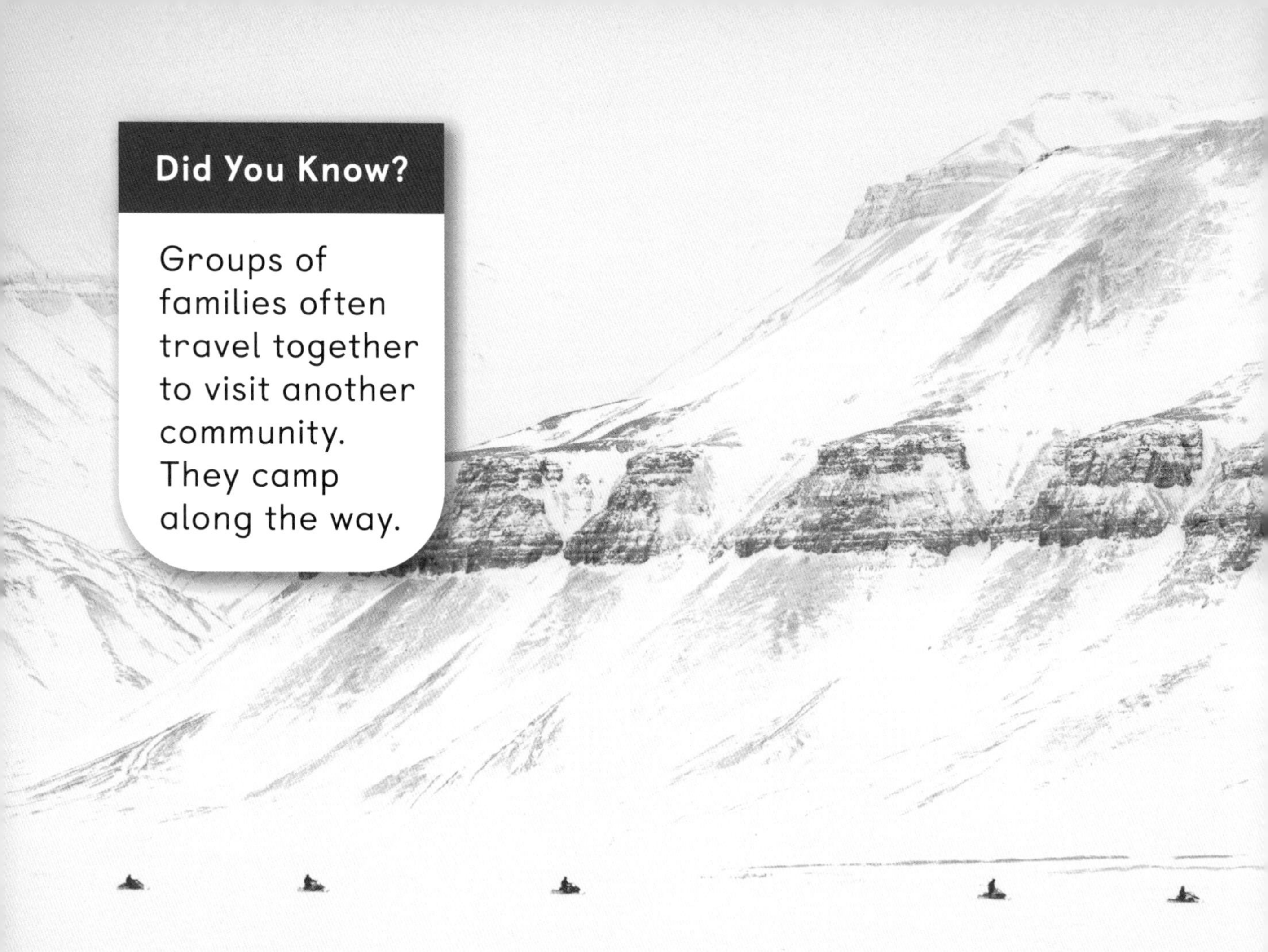

Did You Know?

Groups of families often travel together to visit another community. They camp along the way.

Snowmobiles are used to go on day trips, to go hunting, or to have races.

Another exciting thing to do is dogsledding. Dogs that are well cared for are happy to pull a sled.

Did You Know?

Canadian Inuit dogs have lived in Nunavut for 4,000 years.

10

Using a dog team is a very peaceful way to travel and experience the land. The dogs seem to love the adventure, too!

It's a lot of fun to go sliding on sleds! People slide down hills on wooden or plastic sleds. Sometimes people even slide on sealskins!

14

Kite skiing is an exciting winter activity. Large areas of sea ice and strong winds make Nunavut a great place for kite skiing. Skiers hold on tight!

Some people love to fish in the winter. They drill a hole through the thick sea ice and catch fish with short poles called jigs.

Hunting is a common activity in the winter. Animals that are hunted in the winter include caribou, seal, walrus, polar bear, muskox, fox, and ptarmigan.

The winter months are the best time to see the northern lights, also known as the aurora borealis. Different colours dance through the sky and are a spectacular sight.

Did You Know?

Expert iglu builders can build an iglu in under 15 minutes!

Some people like to build iglus in the winter. They use a saw and a snow knife to cut blocks of snow.

Nunavut is an exciting place to live in and to visit, especially in the winter!